MAIN LINE STEAM SINCE 1984

Images & Words
by
Nick Harrison

BOOK LAW PUBLICATIONS

Dedidcated to:

My wife June, family and friends who have tolerated my hobby since 1984, and to all owners and support crews who have spent many thousands of pounds and hours ensuring that the locomotives continue to operate into the 21st century.

First published in the United Kingdom by Book Law Publications
382 Carlton Hill, Nottingham, NG4 1JA.
Printed and bound in the UK by The Amadeus Press, Cleckheaton, West Yorkshire.

INTRODUCTION

The twenty years that I have been following and photographing steam locomotives all around the United Kingdom has given me a great amount of pleasure. Not only have I had the good fortune of seeing the country as a whole, in all seasons and in all weather conditions, but I have met many other like-minded people who also enjoy the wonders of man made machines working in their intended environment. There is always good camaraderie between us, as well as a competitive spirit as to where and when the best results can be obtained. On many occasions after the main event has finished there is also time to socialise.

During these years, spanning three decades, I have mainly travelled with three groups of friends. In the eighties' I would join company with Ross Middleton and then drive up to Doncaster station where we would meet Pete Thomas who had travelled up from London. After a day on the Settle & Carlisle we would return Pete to Doncaster for his journey home.

Towards the end of the eighties' and into the early nineties', I joined my friends Karl Jauncey and Dave Richards who over the years have put together what is arguably the best video coverage of main line steam available.

Since the mid nineties' I have generally travelled with Brian Dean who I have known for more than twenty years. One of Brian's passions is to be first at a location, and this has led to numerous occasions when we have waited many hours for the train to appear. The record, so far, is six and 1/4 hours at the side of Loch Awe through torrential rain, howling gales, and eventually low evening sun light.

I have estimated that during this twenty year period I have travelled well in excess of 300,000 miles in the pursuit of "the perfect picture", and in that time I have had a couple of near escapes, one when I slipped over and ended up with twelve stitches in a cut when I returned home. On another occasion, whilst travelling to Fort William, a deer made a good attempt at writing-off the car on Rannoch moor.

It goes without saying that the images I have captured and illustrated in this book would not have been possible without the ongoing efforts of many owners, engineers and volunteers who dedicate many hours of their time restoring and maintaining the locomotives and rolling stock to a superb standard.

Nick Harrison
Hucknall, October 2004.

4

(*opposite*) **Former Great Western mixed traffic 'Hall' No.5972 OLTON HALL crossing Ribblehead viaduct on a northbound Settle & Carlisle special. My location for this Saturday 18th December 1999 picture is approximately two-thirds of the way up Whernside's eastern slope, looking towards Penyghent, the crags and snow filled gullies of which can be seen on the skyline about eight miles distant.**

(*right*) **KINLET HALL, No.4936, is seen slogging its way up to Frampton Mansell, between Stroud and Swindon, with a summer special on Sunday 18th June 2000. This 'Hall' is based at Tyseley and can be seen regularly out on the main line. Except for the 57XX 0-6-0PT, the mixed traffic 'Halls' comprised the largest class on the former Great Western Railway and the large number in preservation somewhat reflects this fact. However, on this day numbers meant nothing as No.4936 stalled just twenty yards after this picture was taken.**

ROOD ASHTON HALL, No 4965, on Sunday 18th April 1999 with a special from Derby at Aynho Junction on its way to Oxford. The line from High Wycombe crosses the Oxford line here via the impressive skew bridge.

A pair of 'Halls', ROOD ASHTON and KINLET, leave Birmingham (Snow Hill) and cross Digbeth viaduct on 2nd March 2001. The skyline of Birmingham has since changed considerably with the redevelopment of the Bull Ring shopping centre. The vantage point for this picture was from the roof of a discarded derelict van at the bottom of a local car park.

Former Southern Railway Class N15 'King Arthur' No.777 SIR LAMIEL, the only one of its class to reach preservation, is seen on 27th December 1984 hauling a northbound excursion over the Settle & Carlisle line at Bell Busk, between Skipton and Hellifield. The engine only took the train as far as Appleby before a diesel locomotive returned south with the stock, retracing its northbound journey.

The snow covered Pennines look over the famous Ribblehead viaduct as the N15 SIR LAMIEL leaves a trail of exhaust over the top of its train as it makes the final climb towards Blea Moor on 27th December 1984.

Running alongside the Grand Union canal between Warwick and Kingswood, the route of the GWR in this part of Warwickshire was more or less dictated by the older water course. Leaning to the super elevation of the curve, 'Castle' No.5029 NUNNEY CASTLE climbs Hatton bank at Budbrook shortly after leaving Warwick, the castle of which can be seen in the background. The low winter light on this Saturday, 9th November 1991 afternoon, enhances the exhaust as the engine gets into its stride on the 1 in 110 incline.

(opposite) The penultimate day of the year 2000 was cold indeed and, with snow covering the surrounding countryside at Tram Inn, No. 4936 KINLET HALL is producing plenty of exhaust on the Welsh Marches. It was en route from Birmingham to Newport where the train reversed before proceeding on to Worcester via Cheltenham and Gloucester.

(left) **Having turned on Hatton triangle, NUNNEY CASTLE takes the line to Hatton at Bearley Junction later in the afternoon of the 9th November 1991, with the return working from Stratford to Paddington. The sun had already set at ground level but the last remnants of its orange glow reflected off the exhaust as the train made its way up the branch.**

(opposite) **On Saturday the 7th April 2001, No.5029 NUNNEY CASTLE double headed No.4936 KINLET HALL on a special from Bristol to Penzance. Well into the final stage of the Cornwall leg, the pair are leaving St Austell and traverse the viaduct at the western end of the station. The remains of the original Brunel viaduct can be seen covered in vegetation in front of the structure used today.**

(opposite) **On Monday 16th April 2001, NUNNEY CASTLE and KINLET HALL, on the return journey from Penzance to Bristol, cross Coombe viaduct on the approach to Saltash. In the background can be seen the naval dockyard at Devonport.**

(right) **During the period of Easter 1998 there was a series of shuttle trains run between Exeter and Newton Abbott. On 13th April Auto-tank No.1450 exits the tunnel at Coryton and passes through Coryton Cove with a train heading for Newton Abbott.**

(left) **The Peppercorn K1, No.2005, climbs to the summit at Tyndrum during the glorious midday of Bonfire Night 1990 on the West Highland line under the snow capped Beinn Dorian (3,524 ft). The engine was making its way back south after completing a season of running between Fort William and Mallaig**

(opposite) **Just a bit further south, at Crainlarich on the same day, the K1 is seen taking water.**

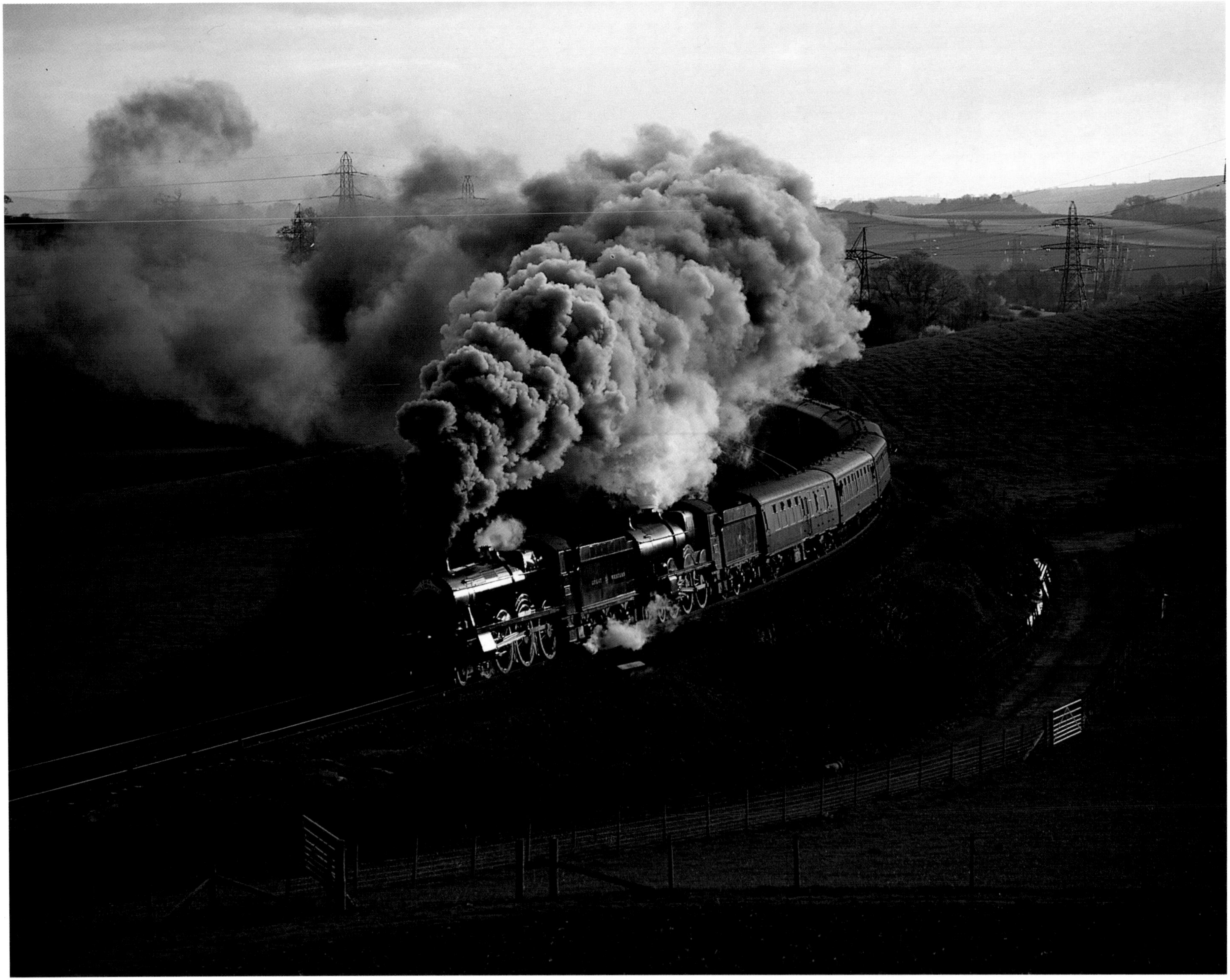

Looking every bit the 'Streak' nickname given to the A4's, No.4498 SIR NIGEL GRESLEY enhances a superb New Years Day in 1993 as it races past Keld on the approach to Appleby with a southbound Settle & Carlisle train comprising a full rake of maroon Mk.1 stock. The exhaust trails the length of the train in the cold afternoon air.

(opposite) Having taken water at Plymouth, after their journey through Cornwall on 16th April 2001, Nos.5029 and 4936 are in full cry on the 1 in 105 of Dainton bank. The sinking sun casts a warm glow onto the exhaust as daylight draws to a close.

Black 5 No 44871 in BR livery, recreates a scene from the early 60,s with a mixed rake of BR MK1 stock as it climbs towards Inverkeithing prior to crossing the Forth Bridge on 31st October 1993.

(opposite) **Immaculately turned out, Pannier No.9600 is seen in the evening light of Sunday 10th June 2001 at Rycroft junction on the return journey from Cosford to Birmingham. The excursion was run by Birmingham Railway Museum to take passengers to the annual air show at Cosford.**

The four cylinder 'Lord Nelson' class consisted of sixteen locomotives which were built between 1926 and 1929. The first of those, No.850 LORD NELSON was retained for preservation and is seen at Hellifield in the summer of 1985 in its Southern livery. The engine has just coupled onto the back of a southbound Settle & Carlisle train and is seen drawing the stock back into Hellifield off the Blackburn branch, ready to take the charter over to Carnforth. This diagram, using two locomotives was a common itinerary in the early 1980's.

(opposite) With a rare morning departure from the Devon town of Newton Abbott, 'King' No.6024 KING EDWARD heads east along the sea wall at Dawlish Warren on 15th February 1995.

Gresley V2 No 4771 GREEN ARROW hauling a full maroon rake of coaches during the summer of 1989. The location is Barron Wood on the Settle & Carlisle line.

(opposite) **'Manor' No.7819 HINTON MANOR reaches terra firma after crossing Barmouth bridge on 16th June 1991, before terminating at Barmouth. Apart from one summer season of 'specials' in 1987, this route has seen very little steam activity since then due to the weak structures on the line. The 'Manor' would feel quite at home on this line, having been associated with this area of Wales since 1943.**

Having stopped at Appleby for water, and 'run pasts' for the train passengers, GREEN ARROW nears the summit of the line at Ais Gill viaduct on that same day in 1989.

Whereas in times past steam locomotives could pick up water from troughs, the modern day railway has no need for such equipment and so preserved steam has to make specific stops to replenish their tenders and tanks. V2 No.4771 is no exception and having again stopped for water, this time at Garsdale, the engine and its train pass over Arten Gill viaduct whilst travelling high up above Dentdale in 1989.

(opposite) **Re-enacting a scene from the late 1950's, rebuilt 'West Country' No.34027 TAW VALLEY passes through Wandsworth Road having left London (Victoria) station over three hours late. This late start in turn opened up the location with the sun having moved round far enough to light the train from the western side. The train later returned to London having travelled via Andover, Salisbury and Southampton. The date was 13th February 1999.**

(right) **On a typical day for weather, under threatening skies on the Settle & Carlisle, 'WC' No.34027 TAW VALLEY powers its train up the final gradient towards Ais Gill summit over Ais Gill viaduct in March 1994.**

On 3rd June 1986 unrebuilt 'West Country' No.34092 CITY OF WELLS hauls a northbound S&C train consisting of a rake of Pullmans with the entire entourage decorated in full *GOLDEN ARROW* regalia.

(opposite) On 14th September 1995, BR Standard Class 4 No.75014, seen at Fassfern with the *JACOBITE*, casts a perfect reflection in the waters of Locheil whilst en route from Fort William to Mallaig.

In former LNER territory but not quite on its usual patch, No.4498 has just left Scarborough on a return working to York and is seen at Seamer Junction in 1987.

(*opposite*) Further down the line, and having stopped at Glenfinnan to pass the normal service train, No.75014 is now skirting the bottom of Lock Eilt with steam to spare whilst en route to Mallaig. Western Scotland certainly has some superb vistas for photography which, when added to the railway aspect, and steam locomotives in particular - produce some wonderful images!

Great Western Railway 4-4-0 No.3440 CITY OF TRURO ran two return trips from York to Scarborough on 20th December 1986 with the *DICKENS FESTIVAL EXPRESS*. The train is on the return run to York at Kirkham Priory.

(opposite) **Running chimney first out of Mallaig, B1 No.61264 is seen skirting Loch Dubh (known as the Black Loch) on 27th September 2001.**

LMS (just) Class 5 No.44767, now named GEORGE STEPHENSON, crossing one of the world's most famous structures - the Forth Railway Bridge - as seen from North Queensferry.

(opposite) BR Standard 8P No.71000 DUKE OF GLOUCESTER. On a rare outing over the Cumbrian coast line, the 'Duke' passes through Millom on its way to Sellafield. 26th October 1996.

In the summer of 1991, the pioneer British Railways Standard locomotive, No.70000 BRITANNIA, made a rare visit over the Settle & Carlisle line and is seen here at Birkett Common.

(opposite) Having failed the previous day to reach its destination, stalling at milepost 19, BR Standard Cl.4 tank No.80079, approaches the summit of the 1 in 80 climb with an excursion from Chester to Blaenau Ffestiniog on 3rd May 1998.

Not able to keep a good un' down, FLYING SCOTSMAN takes an ECS working to Tyseley from Leeds on 27th December 1985. This location is now the station for the Meadow Hall shopping centre on the outskirts of Sheffield.

(opposite) As part of the 125 year celebrations to mark the opening of the West Highland Railway a 'double header' consisting of K1 No.2005 and K4 THE GREAT MARQUIS stopped at every station on the route to Fort William. With the train running very late and having waited on the moor for $6^1/_2$ hours I captured the pair on film crossing Rannoch viaduct in fine style on 7th August 1994.

Making white smoke this time, No.70000 BRITANNIA is seen in the winter of 1992 at the bottom of Hatton Bank with a northbound working.

(opposite) **On the day when A2 No.60532 BLUE PETER should have returned to Aberdeen, the severe early morning frosts of Sunday 17th October 1993 delayed the crossing of the Forth Bridge due to frozen points. Subsequent further delays in the arrival at Perth, meant that had the train continued to Aberdeen, it would have already been dark, giving an arrival time back into Edinburgh the following day. The tour was thus terminated at Perth and returned to Edinburgh via Stirling. The A2 is seen leaving Stirling only minutes before the setting sun disappeared behind local buildings. The bowed signal is not a result of picture distortion - it actually is bent.**

BR Standard Cl.4 No.75069 leaves the former Midland station at Nottingham with a summer special to Matlock in 1987. The building behind the train, the former goods depot, has now been demolished and replaced by a modern building housing the County Courts.

(opposite) During the period between Christmas and New Year what better way could there be to spend a day than travelling through some of Britain's best scenery? On 29th December 1999, V2 No.60800 GREEN ARROW is on the first leg of its journey from Blackburn to Carlisle at Gisburn.

A3 No.4472 is seen at Hope in the spring of 1984 with a movement special which took the engine south to work a train out of London.

(opposite) **Having stopped for water GREEN ARROW and its train are again seen on 29th December, this time at Horton in Ribblesdale. The slopes of Penyghent can be seen in the background with the low winters light catching the train as it climbs the "Long Drag" up towards Ribblehead.**

(opposite) **26th September 1997. On what has proved to be one of the best 'end of season' visits to the West Highland extension, 'Black 5' No.44767 GEORGE STEPHENSON, one of the last LMS built Class 5's, takes the steep climb up the 1 in 48 Beasdale bank in its stride. Built in December 1947 and being allocated initially to Crewe North shed until February 1950, this engine then spent the next fourteen years working from Lancashire sheds, Bank Hall up to March 1962 then Southport until November 1964. Its final move to Kingmoor, from where it was withdrawn in December 1967, gave it the longevity required to get it into the hands of preservationists.**

(right) **On 22nd November 1997 steam at last returned to the Lickey incline south of Birmingham in the shape of two double-headed moguls. With a load of nine coaches, ex LMS Stanier No.2968 and ex GWR Collett No.7325 breast the summit of the 1 in 37 two-mile climb in fine style.**

(opposite) **B1 No.61264 and BR Standard No.75014.** After completing a season on the West Highland extension the pair are seen on an excursion to Oban returning to Crainlarroch some three miles from Oban station on 24th September 2000.

(right) **Stanier's masterpiece No.46229 DUCHESS OF HAMILTON** makes light work of the 1 in 110 climb up to Standedge as it makes its way through Mossley on 30th March 1996.

Back on the S & C on the first day of 1993, the exLNER A4 SIR NIGEL GRESLEY is leaving Helm tunnel whilst running a southbound working.

(*opposite*) On 10th May 2003, Stanier 8F No.48151 took a special from Preston for a day out in Scarborough. Having stopped to allow passengers to board the train at Accrington the train traverses the viaduct which spans the centre of the town.

Of the preserved A4's able to carry out main line work, No.4468 MALLARD is the only one fitted out in the original guise of this class i.e. with full skirting. During the late 1980's this engine was given the chance to run a total of twenty-five trips on the main line and did quite a few of them working out of London. It is seen here on a trip in 1987 to Stratford-on-Avon and is climbing Hatton bank near Warwick.

(opposite) On a rather crisp Tuesday the 25th February 2003, NUNNEY CASTLE was observed climbing the 1 in 115 bank up to White Ball tunnel.

When the Royal Train was steam hauled for the first time since 1967, the honours fell to 'Princess Coronation' class No.6233 DUCHESS OF SUTHERLAND which is seen here getting into its stride across Anglesey at Valley on Tuesday 11th June 2002. Her Majesty The Queen was being taken to Llanfairpwllgwyngyllgogerychwrndrobwllllantysiliogogogoch as part of her Jubilee tour of Great Britain.

(opposite) On 1st February 2003, 'Castle' No.5029 NUNNEY CASTLE took an excursion from Bristol to Penzance. It is seen crossing a typical Cornish style viaduct on the outskirts of Liskeard.

(left) **On 16th October 1994 the Peppercorn K1 ran a special charter, which was marketed for the enthusiast who paid the normal fare for the run, but the train had extra stops built into the itenary which enabled the photographers to pass the train by road and capture the run at numerous locations. Having crossed the viaduct the train makes its way up to the Glenfinnan station in fine style.**

(opposite) **Having stopped at various points along the line, No.2005 and its train is seen again on the 16th October 1994, this time passing the rock face (a location favoured by W.J.V.Anderson) at Lochailort.**

Having worked the train out to Holyhead earlier in the day, Stanier 'Jubilee' No.45596 BAHAMAS looks at home in BR green and with a full rake of maroon BR Mk.1 coaches in tow. It is passing through Valley on 10th October 1993, just five miles into its return journey across Anglesey, en route to Chester.

(opposite) After leaving Blackburn, ex LMS Stanier Mogul No.2968 and its train are seen in the superb countryside of north Lancashire. The town of Burnley can be seen in the distance as the 2-6-0 climbs towards Copy Pit with a York bound special on 8th March 1997.

(opposite) **Having joined its train at Lostock Hall on 22nd July 1992, No.6201 PRINCESS ELIZABETH is seen on a northbound run over the S&C. Due to fire risk the engine had been piloted by a diesel over the "Long Drag" but having completed all the hard work, the diesel was removed at Kirby Stephen. Unbeknown at the time we had decided to try something different on this day and opted for the downhill location of Smardale viaduct.**

(right) **Tunstead quarry in the Peak District with numerous 8F 2-8-0s coming and going with empty and fully loaded trains of hoppers were a common sight up to the end of steam on BR. To celebrate the opening of a new Hopper Loader, the quarry company hired Stanier 8F No.48151 to recreate the past on 11th November 1995. Having collected the rake of ICI hoppers, the 8F pulls the 970 ton pay load towards Great Rocks on a very atmospheric day.**

The ex LNER A3 No.4472 FLYING SCOTSMAN does not figure largely in these pages but it must be included if only for its pioneering main line runs as a preserved locomotive in the earliest days when the number of locomotives capable of carrying out such duties could be counted on one hand. Anyway here, in the winter of 1987, No.4472 is seen at Heyford on its journey from Marylebone to Stratford on Avon.

(opposite) After spending the 1998 season at Fort William, 8F No.48151 made a tour to Inverness where it was based to work an excursion to the Kyle of Lochalsh. Having travelled tender first out to Kyle on 4th October 1998, in dull weather, the 8F returned to Inverness in bright sunshine. The train is seen here leaving Kyle of Lochalsh with the Cuillin hills on the Isle of Skye dominating the horizon.

Built by the LMS in 1925 to complement six other 1914 Derby-built 2-8-0s working on the Ex Somerset & Dorset Joint Railway, LMS 7F No. 53809 is on the return working from Carnforth to Leeds at Kettlesbeck during an early summer evening in 1986.

(opposite) **Stanier Cl.5 No.45407 and Cl.8F No.48773, 17th April 1999. Steam over Copy Pit has not been too plentiful over the last thirty years, in fact rare would be perhaps a better word to use, but on that April day in 1999 the pair of ex LMS engines made a fine sight as they tackled the steep climb over Lydgate viaduct.**

ExLMS 8F No.48151 working a Derby to Buxton special on 24th October 1987 approaches Ambergate Junction.

(opposite) **Having travelled down from London earlier in the day, rebuilt 'West Country' No.34027 TAW VALLEY heads back to the capital through Grateley ten miles after leaving Salisbury on 28th February 1998.**

Seen in its more familiar Brunswick green livery, and now with its BR number, former LMS 'Jubilee' No.45596 BAHAMAS passes Lenton Lane Junction when working a series of shuttles between Nottingham and Derby in the spring of 1989.

(opposite) As the daylight draws to a close, Stanier mogul No.2968 passes Blea Moor signal box on its way up towards Blea Moor tunnel with a northbound S&C, four days before Christmas 1996.

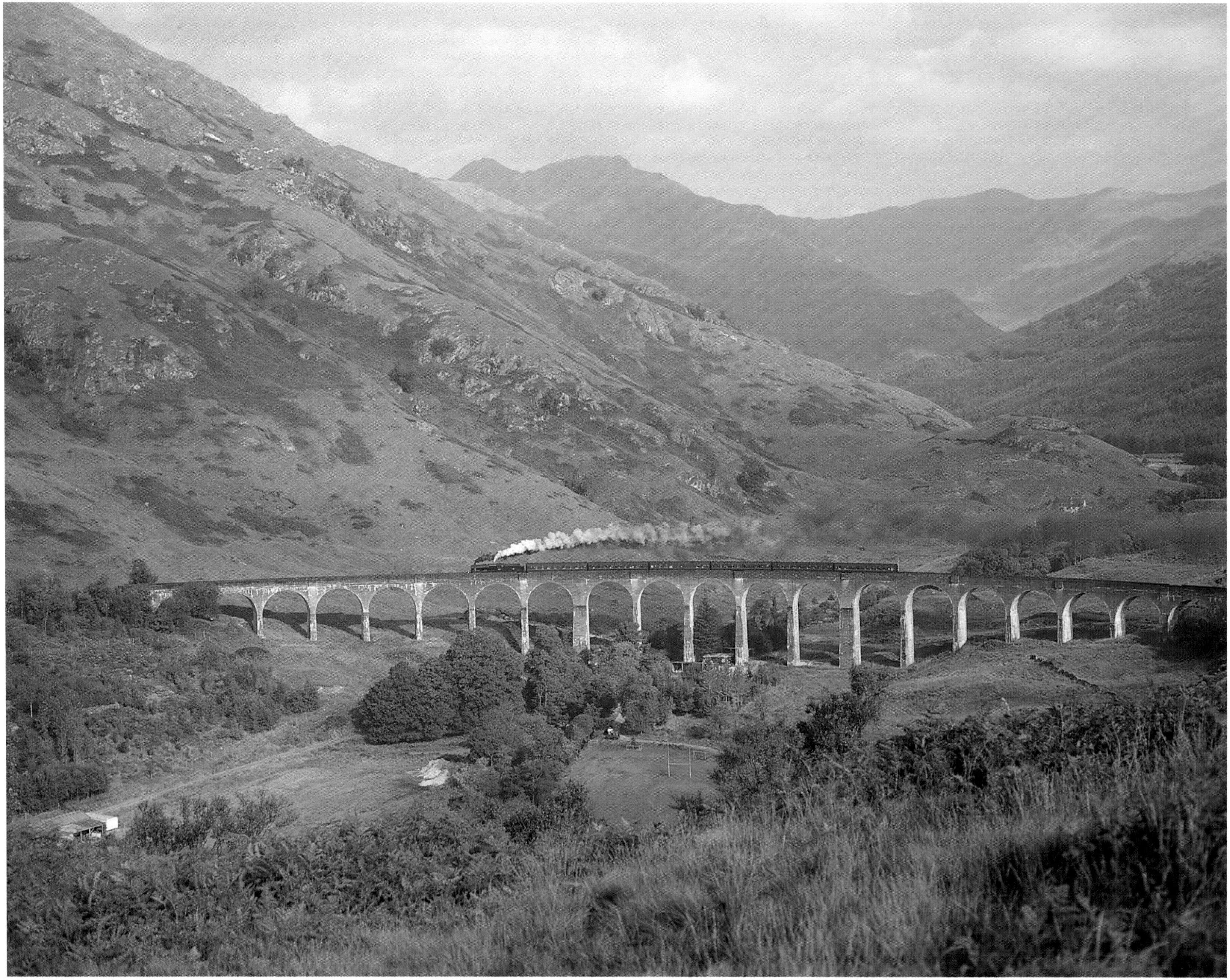

Stanier 'Black 5' No.45407 passes through the award winning station at Hebden Bridge on the Calder valley line on 27th March 1999.

(opposite) **As the season of 'Jacobite' specials nears completion, 8F No.48151 crosses Glenfinnan viaduct on 24th September 1998.**

LMS 'Black 5' No 5305 is one of the many of that class which is preserved (whatever happened to the real Caprotti engines?) and is passing through Gargrave between Skipton and Hellifield on its journey north from Leeds to Carlisle on the 8th March 1986.

(opposite) 'Princess Royal' No.46203 PRINCESS MARGARET ROSE, which is based at Butterley ran an excursion from Derby to Carlisle on the 2nd January 1995. Running almost two hours late, the train emerges from Milford tunnel north of Derby.

(left) In perhaps familiar surroundings, at least during the first couple of years of the 1960's, No.46203 races along the North Wales coast line at Abergele, en route to Holyhead on 16th January 1994.

(opposite) On what used to be a popular route for steam in the 1980's, 'Princess Royal' No.6201 PRINCESS ELIZABETH, skirts the Cumbrian coast at Parton on 5th October 1991, with a return working to Carnforth. Due to the restricted clearances along this stretch of coastal railway, excursions tend to terminate at Sellafield where servicing and turning facilities are available. This also means that these excursions can be operated with just one locomotive whereas an excursion going onto Workington required two locomotives to be used. Note the signal gantry weathered by sea salt.

(opposite) **As part of the 'Rail Festival' in 2003, the Peppercorn K1 No.62005 running as 62052, took an excursion from Fort William to Oban on the 8th October. It was highlighted by the late afternoon sun as it crossed the girder bridge at the end of Loch Awe, near Kilburn Castle, on its return to Fort William.**

(right) **8F No 48151 leaves Carnforth with an excursion for Scarborough on 25th September 1993. The semephore signal has long since gone with the modernisation of the signalling in this area of the country.**

Having turned on Chinley triangle, KALHAPUR is on the return working (25th April 1987) slogging hard up to Peak Forest having just passed Great Rocks Junction.

(opposite) **On 12th March 2004, Thompson B1 No.61264 travelled from Doncaster to Scarborough and back. The return route was via Bridlington and Hull, which has not seen much steam traffic since the early 1960's. With a fully authentic combination of maroon coaching stock and a BR liveried Eastern Region engine, the train, having been stopped at Hunmanby, accelerates up the 1 in 102 gradient towards the summit at Speeton.**

On its first run south over the S&C after restoration to main line running, A2 No.60532 BLUE PETER is at full stretch as it powers it's way towards Kirby Stephen at Waitby on 21st March 1992.

(opposite) 'King' No.6024, on 9th November 1995, speeding past the locks at one of the most famous Great Western system scenes alongside the Kennet and Avon canal at Great Bedwyn.

In late summer of 2001, the green vegetation was starting to change colour as V2 No.60800 GREEN ARROW passes Selside on a northbound journey over the S&C on the 8th September. Storm clouds and Penyghent dominate the background.

On 6th March 1993, the 60532 travelled both ways over the Settle & Carlisle line. Here it crosses Smardale viaduct with the return run in the early evening light.

Catching the last rays of the setting sun at Haxby, on the 20th December 1986, CITY OF TRURO is on its second run of the *DICKENS FESTIVAL EXPRESS*.

No.46229 DUCHESS OF HAMILTON on the last trip that it made prior to withdrawal for a major overhaul in October 1985. The engine is seen hauling a southbound S&C working at Barron Wood.

Another setting sun catches MALLARD at Bearley Junction on its return journey from Stratford-on-Avon to London in 1987.

Having finished the season on the Fort William to Mallaig line, K1 No.2005 heads home on 22nd October 1994 with a special to Glasgow. Having successfully climbed through Monessie Gorge the engine rounds the curve at Tulloch before starting the ascent to Corrour.

(opposite) **After taking water at Long Preston, 'Princess Royal' No.46203 PRINCESS MARGARET ROSE takes the route towards Skipton having passed through the restored station at Hellifield on 19th March 1994.**

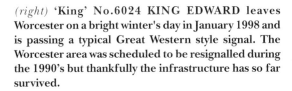

(right) **'King' No.6024 KING EDWARD leaves Worcester on a bright winter's day in January 1998 and is passing a typical Great Western style signal. The Worcester area was scheduled to be resignalled during the 1990's but thankfully the infrastructure has so far survived.**

Former LMS 'Jubilee' No.5593 KALHAPUR crosses Sheriffs Brow with a northbound S&C working on 21st March 1987.

(opposite) Wearing its LMS period livery, Stanier Cl.5 No.5407 is running on the former Glasgow & South Western route and is crossing Stewarton viaduct some six miles north of Kilmarnock on 4th January 1992.

FLYING SCOTSMAN is highlighted by the setting sun at Whitehouse Farm in December 1986 whilst working a *SANTA SPECIAL* from High Wycombe to London.

Every time I travelled north up the M1 motorway I always thought it would be nice to have the opportunity to witness a steam train passing through Pinxton on the climb up to Kirkby-in-Ashfield. On 16th January 1999, Stanier 8F No.48773 made a tour of the Nottinghamshire coal lines giving the opportunity to record this scene which has now disappeared with the old slag heap being sold and the collieries along the line closed and demolished.

'Castle' No.5051 EARL BATHURST leaves Bristol Temple Meads, en route for Kingswear, on Saturday 5th September 2004. The fireman is working overtime to obscure the early morning sunlight. Formerly DRYSLLWYN CASTLE, this engine lost that name to fellow class member No.7018 in the 1950's.